Teaching the Craft of Writing

Ideas

by Lola M. Schaefer

New York • Toronto • London • Auckland • Sydney
Mexico City • New Delhi • Hong Kong • Buenos Aires

Dedication

For young writers everywhere

Acknowledgments

I appreciate these teachers who shared their insights as well as samples of student work:

* Marolyn Krauss at Horizon Elementary School

* Michele LaFever and Carolyn Fletcher at South Adams Elementary School

* Heather Fox and Hilary Hamman at Pierceton Elementary School

* Jaime Brunson at J. E. Ober Elementary School

* Darla Kingrey and Ann Hollar at Horace Mann Elementary School

Thank you to my editors, Joanna and Sarah, who both continue to be a source of inspiration and support.

And, I offer my sincere gratitude to student writers, who willingly experiment and tell us what works best for them.

✳ ✳ ✳

Cover Design by Maria Lilja
Cover Illustration by Kristen Balouch
Interior Design by Sarah Morrow

Copyright © 2006 by Lola M. Schaefer
All rights reserved.
Published by Scholastic Inc.
Printed in the U.S.A.
ISBN 0-439-44399-7

2 3 4 5 6 7 8 9 10 40 11 10 09 08 07 06

Table of Contents

Introduction

For the past eight years, I have been a visiting writing coach in elementary and middle schools. During my residencies, the students and I create our own original pieces of writing from an initial idea through revision. During this three- to five-day writing process, we are constantly working on craft. Craft is the art of using tools and skills to produce meaningful text.

As I work with student writers, I envision that each of them has a writing backpack. Our job as teachers is to provide students with strategies that become life-long tools they can carry with them in these backpacks. How do we do this? We first create a non-threatening writing community where teacher and students experiment with words, side by side. Next, we offer students a rich environment of published literature, modeling, demonstration, practice (lots of practice), and a receptive audience.

What is so encouraging is that I watch student writers embrace these strategies and quickly improve in the craft of writing. Since writing is a form of self-expression, it only makes sense that they would want to know how to do the following:

- use and maintain a writer's notebook
- select and refine an idea
- organize for different purposes and genres
- add interest and information through elaboration
- develop a genuine writer's voice
- write strong leads that lure readers into the text
- create endings that satisfy readers
- revise the piece until it reflects their intent

I believe that students' attention and commitment are strong because they are practicing craft in the context of their own authentic work. Involvement is always more active when writers are able to self-select their topics. They have something to say that is important to them—something they believe and care about. The writing has a purpose, and the strategies hold promise to help students realize that purpose.

Teaching craft is more a journey of discovery rather than a precise, step-by-step program. Student writers need to be immersed in a constant study of how other authors craft their work. They need to study published writing such as poetry, story, nonfiction, and memoir. They need well-focused mini-lessons that act as constant reminders of what craft is and what it can do. They need time to reflect, plan, draft, rethink, draft again, revise, and share.

Most important, our student writers need encouragement and support. Celebrate everything they write well. Then, watch your students express themselves in ways you never thought possible.

Chapter 1

What Is an Idea?

Introducing Students to Writing Ideas

Webster's dictionary tells us that an idea is a conception existing in the mind as a result of mental activity; a plan. For me, a writing idea is a spark. Sometimes it follows creative thinking, but quite often, it seems to come out of nowhere. In fact, of all my writing ideas, the most intriguing and inviting ones are those that appear unannounced. I've been struck with writing ideas while gardening, driving, walking, reading, and, of course, falling asleep. A writing idea is a gentle push to research, explore, and reflect. It demands attention. It's the impulse to write.

Today, I was working with second-grade students who write daily, so I asked them, "What's a writing idea?" Here are some of their thoughts.

- "It's what you write and draw about."
- "It's that thing that keeps your writing going on and on."
- "To get a good idea you need to take time to think."
- "It's the fun part—the part that makes me love to write."

I can relate to all of these statements, but the last one especially. Often, it is that initial idea that fills me with determination and joy. I want to realize it in final form so badly that I'm willing to think, plan, write, revise, rethink, revise, sometimes for weeks, sometimes for months. But that initial idea is the impetus that keeps me motivated. Watching an idea come to life makes all the work worthwhile.

That's an explanation from the inspirational viewpoint of what an idea is. As important as that understanding is, there's more to a writing idea. An idea is the keystone of good writing. I don't mean the ideas that are thrown at writers as prompts but the ideas that bubble up from who the writers are, what they care about, and what they know or want to know. Ideas that have their basis in emotion, knowledge, or a keen interest motivate writers. Those ideas push writers forward as they work with words to find just the right way to express themselves. That's why we work with student writers. We are developing independent writers who will have the tools to express themselves for the rest of their lives.

We teachers need to help students find their most powerful ideas. It takes time to learn how to mine an idea that holds emotional impact for us, the writers—enough of an impact to sustain us through the writing process. Once writers are involved in daily writing, they need an ongoing supply of ideas. We need to show students through our own modeling and the reading of published works how to select ideas that will motivate them to be the best writers they can be.

An Idea Is Not a Topic

Ideas are different than topics. A topic is a general subject—like dogs, soccer, birthdays, ice-skating, jungle animals, the ocean, stars, babysitters, computers, backyard games, amusement parks, the Rocky Mountains, or food. Quite often, teachers and students brainstorm lists of topics that interest them and display the responses in their classrooms.

These topics are not meant to be writing ideas. They are simply categories of interest. In fact, if students try to write on one of these topics, their writing will usually lack organization. Topics are too general and vague to offer the focus students need to write well.

A writing idea is much more specific. Typical writing ideas could be an explanation of the advantages and disadvantages of the giraffe's long neck; how six weeks of soccer camp paid off with a surprising play in the first game of the season; a poem about butterflies and how they move; how easy it is to lose track of time while working on the computer; the role of a tennis coach; how dolphins communicate; what I like about my best friend; the joys and challenges of writing; how I got my dog. Ideas have a focus. Before sitting down to write, the writer knows what he or she wants to say to an audience. Ideas provide purpose.

Do ideas change during development? You bet! In fact, most writers will tell you that's part of the charm. You can start writing with a basic plan of where you're headed, and then inspiration sneaks in to provide a clearer understanding of what you want to say. It's a gift when that happens, and I've watched it surprise many student writers. This inspiration and understanding almost always happens while they're writing, thinking, or sharing. The refined idea doesn't just spring into a writer's mind completely honed. It usually comes in dribbles and spits while a writer works. Thinking and probing deeper into the narrative, description, or information leads the writer to the core of the idea.

Ideas Take Shape

J. Patrick Lewis is a published children's poet and author. His choice of writing ideas covers such interesting topics as planet Earth, praisesongs, geographic travels, and math riddle-rhymes.

Lewis shares this about his process:

Ideas rarely come from a willing Muse. They are cobbled together at the anvil of the lonely writer's trade, that is, by sitting for long hours in a chair staring at a blank screen. If the Muse speaks to me, she usually does so through books I am reading—so many ideas are generated by what others have written, or in memories from childhood—my own or my children's, or in closely watching people, animals, events. And then the idea evolves as you are working it out by playing with words, which is happily my full-time occupation.

At www.jpatricklewis.com, you can catch a glimpse of Mr. Lewis and a few of his latest books.

Chapter 1 Review

- Ideas are the keystone of good writing.
- A strong writing idea will sustain an author through the writing process.
- Topics are general subjects for writing; they are not ideas.
- Ideas have a specific focus and purpose.
- Ideas can change as a writer works.

Chapter 2

Finding Ideas in Everyday Life
Helping Students Develop Ideas

It is my good fortune to work with many elementary and middle school students each year, both as a writing consultant and a visiting author in schools. I find that young writers are eager. They want to share what's important to them through their writing. They want to learn how other writers work, and they are anxious to learn how to improve their writing.

Quite often, I am asked into schools to speak with students, author to authors. I love those visits. Before I begin explaining my process as a writer, or where I find inspiration for new ideas, I always ask the following question: "What are some of your favorite books?"

I like to learn which books have an impact on students. It gives me background on who they are as readers and writers. I am intrigued with the correlation between what children read and what they write. Using this informal survey, I've noticed a pattern. In schools where students are continually exposed to a variety of genres and titles and are provided time to read broadly and write about self-selected ideas, they speak enthusiastically about books and reading and writing. This isn't surprising, you might say. Yet their attitude is revealing. It shows us that the first step in creating lifelong readers and writers is an environment that offers a wide range of the best of children's literature. Such an environment needs knowledgeable instructors who can lead students into these books with purpose and passion. We can safely say that young writers are first young readers.

 ## Where Do Young Writers Get Their Ideas?

The second question I ask during these author to authors exchanges is "Where do you get your writing ideas?" (I'm beating students to the punch because if I don't ask them, they inevitably ask me this question.) Most authors, and many teachers, think that schoolchildren ask this question because they have a difficult time finding ideas for themselves. I disagree. I believe they are seeking confirmation that all writers find ideas in many of the same ways: from families, friends, and pets; books; activities and personal interests; imagination; and observations.

 ## Ideas from Home

One of the first replies that I always hear to my question about writing ideas is this: "I get my ideas from my family and my pet." Of course, all writers know the value in mining the emotional events that happen in our own families: reunion mischief, the birth of a brother, the loss of a pet, helping a sister get ready for college, camping at the beach, visiting a grandparent in the hospital or senior center, or missing the championship baseball game. There is an endless supply of writing ideas right inside our own homes and personal lives.

How Do Other Authors Get Their Ideas?

In *The ABC's of Writing for Children*, Elizabeth Koehler-Pentacoff has compiled an exhaustive book of quotations and interviews on the art and craft of writing children's literature. Share this expert advice from 114 children's authors with your students. Read how these writers receive inspiration and find their ideas. Koehler-Pentacoff's book will provide insight, opinions, and validation for your student writers. They will learn how other authors tackle the writing process from first idea to final draft.

Don't be surprised if your students find quotations in the book that they want to copy or hang in the classroom. One of the greatest supports writers can have is learning they are not alone.

Where Do Published Authors Get Their Ideas?

Linda Oatman High, author of young adult and middle grade novels, picture books, and poetry for children, enjoys working on a variety of books at the same time. When asked where she gets her ideas, Ms. High explains:

Real life, past and present, explodes with ideas. I keep journals all over my house in which to capture the ideas. Ideas for two of my books came from real life. Barn Savers—based on my husband's job of recycling old barns—came from everyday life. The Girl on the High-Diving Horse— based on the old Atlantic City act—came from my childhood memories of seeing the horses dive from the sky.

Visit Linda Oatman High's Web site at www.lindaoatmanhigh.com to see what's new in her life.

Start with Family

Use the home and family as a starting place for ideas on the first day of school. Reserve a portion of a bulletin board as your classroom notebook. Ask students the following kinds of questions to help them brainstorm writing ideas for the future:

- What's your favorite place in your home?
- Do you have a pet? Where did you get it? How did you decide on a name?
- How does your household wake up?
- What's your favorite holiday celebration?
- What kinds of animals live in your yard?
- What are the busiest times in your house?
- What kinds of things does your mother (father) help you do?
- Have you ever been afraid in your home? What happened?
- Where's your favorite hiding place at home?
- What does your sister (brother) do that makes you giggle?
- What does your sister (brother) do that irritates you?
- What are your bedtime rituals? What do you do before going to bed?

To get the most involvement from your students, you want to ask questions that relate to their basic emotions. It's easy to remember events or happenings that center around fear, happiness, sadness, comfort, excitement, embarrassment, frustration, or pride because that's how all of us mentally file our past experiences—by an emotional connection. Students can easily recall experiences when questioned this way because we're tapping into two familiar areas—home and emotions.

Not all students will have answers to every question. That's fine. The purpose of this short exercise is not to write about the exact question but to brainstorm specific areas of interest that later can be shaped into solid writing ideas. Don't be surprised if your students branch off from your questions and offer ideas on what's important to them about their homes.

Students may want to make a few notes about their writing ideas on small squares of paper to post on the bulletin board, or you may act as the scribe and post their ideas for them.

 ## Ideas from Books

Another ready response from students about writing ideas is "I get my ideas from other books." I immediately ask them this follow-up question: "Do you mean you write about some of the same topics that you read about in books, or does your mind fill with new ideas?" Right away, students tell me that they never write about the same topics that are in the books, but in some mysterious way, reading sparks their imagination—they come up with lots of things to write about. (Additional discussion on books and ideas is offered in Chapter 3.)

Boy, can I relate! One of my greatest joys is to take a day off and go to the local library or bookstore. I sit on the floor by the picture books and read and read and read. New writing ideas flood my mind. I keep my writer's notebook open at my side so I can record ideas as they materialize. Again, my ideas, like the students' ideas, don't seem to be connected to the books I've read. It's as if losing myself in other authors' words releases a wealth of ideas that have been resting in my subconscious. When I share this with the students, they nod in understanding. We're talking the same language. I'm confirming that their method of discovering new writing ideas is the same as mine, a published author. That feels good!

Ideas from Activities

A great many students respond to my question by saying, "I write about things I do." These students like to write school stories and accounts of basketball camp or dance class. They know the terminology, setting, dialogue, and problems that they've witnessed during those experiences. I immediately let students know that published authors also write about what they have seen, heard, and experienced.

I explain that published authors sometimes write dog stories or poems because they have lived with dogs and have observed their behavior for many years. Other authors write soccer stories because they watch and enjoy the sport or they coach a soccer team. Authors who write about gardening also grow flowers and vegetables and want to share that experience with their readers. I always tell students that authors need to write about what they know and care about because those pieces will be their strongest writing.

Read and Record

One year, my students and I hung several sheets of chart paper on the wall in the reading center. This giant pad had two purposes. First, students wanted to write their reflections about books where others could read them and respond. This turned out to be one of those grand ideas that came from the students themselves. They enjoyed this ongoing dialogue about their literature, and so did I.

The second purpose for this wall tablet was to have an available space to record writing ideas when they popped into students' heads. They, too, were bombarded with good ideas when engaged in reading. As stated before, these weren't necessarily copycat ideas but original ideas that sprang from the subconscious as students read. This purpose sustained itself for one grading period, and then slowly students began taking their writers' notebooks with them to the reading center so they could keep a private record of their ideas. It's not that they didn't want others reading their ideas, but they felt such an ownership that they wanted to record the ideas in their own notebooks. Also by then, students were in the habit of adding notes and details to their original ideas, and their individual notebooks afforded them a better place to do this. (See Chapter 4 for more information about writers' notebooks.)

I suggest starting the year with some sort of a scrapbook or notebook in the reading center so students will have a notebook close by when an idea pops into their heads. It's so satisfying to be able to write down an idea as soon as it appears. Later, students can reread these ideas and transfer those that still appeal to them to their notebooks.

Ideas from Personal Interests

Along with family and home, I always want to learn about my students' interests as soon as possible. Again, you can add more writing ideas to your bulletin board notebook by asking your students about their hobbies and extra-curricular interests. For instance, you might ask the following questions:

- Does anyone collect rocks? stamps? baseball cards? coins? dolls? fossils? arrowheads? books? What's your favorite item in your collection? Where did you get it?

- Does anyone play a musical instrument? Do you take lessons? How long have you played? Do you have music recitals? How do you feel on those days?

- Does anyone belong to a club? Boy or Girl Scouts? an after-school group? How often do you meet? What do you do that you like?

- Does anyone make jewelry or sew? Does someone crochet or knit?

- Is anyone a movie buff? What's your favorite movie and why?

- Does someone draw or make cartoons? How did you first get started?

Again, the goal is not to have every child answer each question or even participate with a response. Our aim is to ignite thinking that will generate personal ideas that students will want to write about.

Ideas from Imagination

Another response some students give me about finding writing ideas is this: "I use my imagination." These are the children who like to make up stories. They enjoy writing adventures, mysteries, and fantasies. And guess what?! When I ask these students what kinds of books they like to read, they always answer with titles that match the genre they enjoy writing the most. They're just not aware yet that these books are fueling their imaginations.

It's fun to share with students that most stories come from someone's imagination. But even our imagination is shaped somewhat by our experience. We tend to imagine within a framework of what we know or think to be possible, entertaining, logical, or interesting.

Out of This World

When helping students brainstorm ideas, don't forget their vivid imaginations. You can remind them of their "out of this world" ideas by asking:

- Do you ever pretend that you can fly?
- If you could live anywhere else, where would it be?
- Do you ever have a dream that you remember?
- If you could be any animal, what would it be?
- When you daydream, what do you think about?

Again, please remember that these are not writing ideas in themselves. These are questions posed to spark authentic ideas in student writers. Some students will only want to write information pieces when given an opportunity. Others will write fictional stories. We need to brainstorm in many different ways to show them that anything is possible in writing.

Ideas from the Real World

At every school there are students who like to write information books. They tell me that they always write about horses, ballet, volcanoes, or the sun. These students are passionate about their latest areas of research. When I ask where they get their new information, they tell me that they watch videos or special TV shows on their topics. They read encyclopedias, online articles, and other information books. Sometimes, they interview people, like their parents or neighbors, who they believe to be experts on specific topics. Quite often, they simply say, "I already know a bunch of stuff about this. That's where my idea came from."

> "I like to write about biking, swimming, and skateboarding. I'm one of those people who writes about real life."
>
> — 2nd grader

When your students are involved in independent research, remind them that when they find an interesting nugget, they can record it in their writer's notebook for future reference. If they are like me, they will find many fascinating facts relating to their topic, and some on entirely different topics, as they explore their resources. All of this input is rich material for writing ideas.

Ideas from Observation

One of the final responses, usually from a quiet and more reflective student, is "Sometimes I see or hear something and that reminds me of what I want to write about." Of course! Aren't we all inspired by the little curiosities that we notice around us? Maybe it's the way the moon is visible in the daytime sky as if it's watching over us, or it could be the flight of a hummingbird as it feeds in a garden. Look at how many people have written about the marvels of the life cycle of a tree, a flower, or an animal. Many common, everyday occurrences take on new meaning when we take the time to sit still and watch. Children find the whole metamorphosis of a caterpillar into a butterfly a remarkable event. They love to write about the transformation. At the other end of the spectrum, some students have observed the rhythm of city traffic and written poems that capture the cadence and sounds of its stop-and-go rhythm.

There Is No Magic Formula

The answers about where students get their ideas vary some from school to school, but never—and I do mean NEVER— have I had a student reply, "I can't think of anything to write about." Yet, when I work with teachers on the writing process, one of the most common complaints I hear is this: "I always have a few students who can never find anything to write about. What do I do with them?"

> *"I get my ideas from my surroundings and the things that happen to me."*
>
> — 4th grader

Look All Around

Many students have a knack for noticing the world around them. Others need to be taught how to be observant. Sometimes just asking a few questions can remind students of something special they've seen. In their minds, they can revisit these scenes and write about them with awe and a distinct voice. To help brainstorm these kinds of moments, you might ask the following questions:

- Have you ever witnessed an animal being born?
- Have you ever taken the time to rest beneath a tree and watch the different animals that visit?
- Have you ever studied a toad or a mouse up close? What did you notice?
- Is there a tree outside your bedroom window that changes with the seasons? Can you describe what happens to the leaves?
- Have you ever gone on a nighttime hike through the woods? What sounds did you hear?
- Have you ever held a newborn baby in your arms? Can you remember what you noticed?
- Have you ever taken a canoe ride down a quiet river? What did you see, hear, or smell?

You can add questions to this list from your own personal experiences. Watch students' eyes light up as they remember these awe-inspiring moments from their pasts.

One of the best presents we can give our students is the understanding that writing ideas are all around us. There is no magic formula that enables some writers to think of more ideas than others. It's just that some people are more observant, more reflective. These writers take their time to think about the world around them and record ideas as they come. As teachers, we need to show students how to notice, record, and mine the many ideas around them.

Chapter 2 Review

- Young writers are first young readers.

- Students can mine writing ideas from their homes and families, books, activities and interests, imaginations, research and knowledge, and observations of the world around them.

- Students need to be trained to recognize writing ideas when they appear.

Chapter 3

Finding Ideas Through Reading and Thinking as a Writer

As I mentioned at the beginning of this book, students gain an appreciation of books and the written word from reading and having books read to them. We begin to fill their idea bank by reading wide and deep. Of course, the first time we read any book, poem, or story to students, the only purpose is pure entertainment and joy. We want to lure them into the world of reading. By the second or third engagement with the book, you can ask targeted questions that will guide students into a discussion of genre, format, information, and ideas. As students reflect on the text, they will spawn their own writing ideas.

When we read aloud we're showing students the literature that they will be reading soon. We speak with expression and cadence. Students hear specific vocabulary and proper syntax in a meaningful context. And, if we select the best literature to share, there will be an emotional impact on the listeners. They might experience a sense of awe or wonder at what they hear and learn, or they might feel anger, empathy, joy, surprise, grief, or fear. Each listener will relate to the text in his or her own personal way.

> *"Most of my ideas come from my imagination."*
>
> — 2nd grader

Every time we read another book or poem or information article, our students are subconsciously realizing that they, too, could write about this topic or something similar. Occasionally, we help that process by asking a few questions. At this stage of the process, when we're trying to help students identify personal writing ideas, we want them to be aware of all the idea possibilities. After reading aloud excellent literature, we can encourage students to think more deeply about whether a book sparks any future writing ideas in them.

Mining Personal Ideas from the Read-Aloud

One of the books I like to use to help students mine personal ideas is the narrative nonfiction book *Waiting for Wings* by Lois Ehlert. After reading the book, I make a few comments and ask some questions to tap into children's affective domain. I want them to make a personal connection with this book. Here's a sample of this.

Mrs. S.:   Did you enjoy this book?

Felix: Yes. I like the different size pages.

Madison: She showed us the whole life cycle of the butterfly and that was great!

Molly: I really liked how at the end the butterflies were flying around.

Mrs. S.:   I love this book. It's one of my favorites. I can't believe how much information the author shares in so few words. Did you learn anything new about this life cycle?

George: Butterfly glue—I didn't know they stuck their eggs on leaves with their own sticky stuff. I liked how she used those words.

Erik: I learned that the chrysalis is torn by the new butterfly.

Felix: I didn't know that new butterflies pumped their wings before they flew.

Leah: I learned that butterflies follow a sweet smell to the flowers.

Mrs. S.:   How many of you think that you'd like to write about an animal or a plant one day? (*Several students raise their hands.*) Tell me what you'd like to write about, please.

Erik: A praying mantis—we had one in our yard last year.

Molly: I'd like to write about mastodons. I know they're extinct, but I still like them.

Tino: I could write about milkweed. That's where Monarch butterflies lay their eggs.

Mrs. S.:   I'm thinking of some writing ideas myself. I like sunflowers and could write about how the birds spread their seeds. We also have two bats living in our old barn. I could write about bats and what they do at night. The pages could be black, and I could print the text in white ink or chalk. I also think it's pretty cool how morning glories climb up poles and fences. I would like to do some research on that flower and write a piece where the words climb up and over things like the morning glories.

Madison: Your idea about bats made me think about raccoons. They always come out at night when we're camping. I'd like to write about how people make too much noise for the raccoons.

As you can see, *Waiting for Wings* can spark a lot of writing ideas in students. It's an exciting book because of its language, illustration, and format. The one thing we want to remember is to read a variety of stories, poems, and articles to students. Fortunately there's a wide range of excellent literature available for children in grades 2–4. However, please make sure that your selections are books and stories that you can share with sincere enthusiasm. We want to light a fire in these young readers and writers.

> ## Picture Books to Generate Writing Ideas
>
> - *A is for Abigail* by Lynne Cheney (information book)
> - *Diary of a Worm* by Doreen Cronin (diary written from a worm's point-of-view)
> - *Earthshake: Poems from the Ground Up* by Lisa Westberg Peters (poetry)
> - *Fossil* by Claire Ewart (discovery of a fossil and the animal that once lived)
> - *The Gardener* by Sarah Stewart (story told through letters)
> - *How Do You Raise a Raisin?* by Pam Munoz Ryan (narrative non-fiction)
> - *How the Elephant Got Its Trunk* by Jean Richards (retelling of a Kipling tale)
> - *Mama Loves* by Rebecca Kai Dotlich (poetic picture book)
> - *On Sand Island* by Jacqueline Briggs Martin (story told in poems)
> - *One Is a Snail, Ten Is a Crab* by April Pulley Sayre (a counting book)
> - *So You Want to Be an Inventor?* by Judith St. George (describes inventors and their inventions)
> - *Today I Feel Silly and Other Moods That Make My Day* by Jamie Lee Curtis (concept book about feelings)

Making an Emotional Connection to a Read-Aloud

Another way I like to help students discover their own writing ideas is by identifying emotional hot spots in the books that we read out loud. For instance, when I read *When Vera Was Sick* by Vera Rosenberry, I assume that almost every child can think of a time when he or she was ill and had to stay home in bed. Just like Vera, the students might have been ill with chicken pox, or have had influenza or strep throat. That's why I select a book that shows an experience common to many children. Some student listeners immediately form a personal connection with the character in the book. Hands go up, and they want to share their stories of past illnesses. This is a wonderful time to help students brainstorm possible writing ideas for the future. Here are some ideas from my work in the classroom:

- the time my whole family was sick with the flu at once
- the awful-tasting cough medicine I had to take when I had bronchitis
- what I like to do when I'm ill in bed
- how my mom or dad spoils me when I'm ill

Not every student will relate to *When Vera Was Sick*, but some will add new entries to their idea banks. I call this approach "Going in the Front Door." We're looking at the main story of the book and deciding if we have similar personal experiences that we might want to share with an audience. It's the first obvious connection we can make with what we've read.

As helpful as this approach is—and it always generates many thoughtful ideas—I often try to find one small part in the story, a common incident, that might conjure up a wider range of responses. As a teacher and parent, it's usually not difficult for me to find these emotional parts for students. In *When Vera Was Sick*, there's a scene near the beginning of the story where Vera cries out to her mom. The text says, "Her tummy ached all over." Of course, in this context we're talking about an upset stomach when someone is ill. (Plus, Vera has been recently frightened by her own imagination.) To make the interpretation broader, I say, "Think about a time when your tummy hurt. What was happening to you?"

After a few moments of contemplation, hands always shoot into the air. Here are some common responses I've heard:

- Once I couldn't find my mom in the mall. My stomach got tight and started to hurt.

- My brother went away to college last year. At night I'd go into his room and sit on his bed. I missed him so much that my stomach hurt for days.

- Last year I almost ate all of my Halloween candy in one night. My stomach hurt real bad.

- I couldn't find my kitten last week. I looked everywhere in our house and outside. My stomach hurt until my dad found her under the porch step.

Books with Child Appeal

Of course, sparking an emotional connection begins with the reading of excellent children's literature—books with which they can relate. It's worthwhile to take the extra time to locate these kinds of books. Here's a short list to add to the titles you already know and love. When you've exhausted these, speak to a local children's librarian. He or she will be able to direct you to many more.

- *Amazing Grace* by Mary Hoffman
- *Freedom Summer* by Deborah Wiles
- *The Girl on the High-Diving Horse* by Linda Oatman High
- *Journey* by Patricia MacLachlan
- *The Memory String* by Eve Bunting
- *Miss Nelson Is Missing* by Harry G. Allard
- *Thank You, Mr. Falker* by Patricia Polacco
- *Vera Runs Away* by Vera Rosenberry
- *When Sophie Gets Angry—Really, Really Angry* by Molly Bang
- *The Relatives Came* by Cynthia Rylant

I call this approach "Going in the Back Door." This tummy-ache scene is just one small fragment of the story, but it's a common emotional response to a fearful, uncomfortable, or unfortunate circumstance. We easily can recall the last time our stomachs hurt, we yelled out, or we jumped for joy. Our brains seem to sort and file our strongest memories by emotional associations. That's why I prefer to generate writing ideas through *emotions*, rather than events. It's easier for most students to brainstorm the important events of their lives if they access ideas this way. Again, not every student is going to relate to this particular stimulus, and that's quite all right because we can provide plenty of other opportunities to find emotional connections as we continue to read and discuss books together.

 ## Mini-Lesson: *Nana Upstairs & Nana Downstairs*

I've also used these front- and back-door approaches to mining writing ideas with *Nana Upstairs & Nana Downstairs* by Tomie dePaola. The following mini-lesson shows how one discussion can smoothly flow between the two strategies. Remember, this discussion would follow the second or third reading of the book, not the first.

Mrs. S.: How many of you have a special grandma or grandpa in your lives? (*Many students raise their hands.*) What was something special that Tommy's Nana downstairs always did?

Nora: She cooked. My grandma bakes for us sometimes. She makes really good pies.

Tino: Nana downstairs took care of Nana upstairs. Sometimes, we have to go over to my grandpa's house and take care of him.

Mrs. S.: Can any of you tell us some of the special things that your grandmas, grandpa, aunts, or uncles do?

Leah: My aunt Molly works in a hospital. She's a nurse.

Isabel: My grandpa is the best gardener. He grows the biggest roses in his neighborhood.

Sam: My uncle Nate can fix anything. He likes to do it and people bring him toasters, cars, lawnmowers, even clocks.

Mrs. S.: Take a few moments and jot some ideas down in your writer's notebook. Would some of you like to write about your grandmas, grandpas, aunts, or uncles? (*Many students nod their heads.*) Maybe you want to think about how your grandma can quilt. Or perhaps one day you'd like to write how your uncle helped you build a go-cart.

When students have jotted down their writing ideas, I turn to the page where Tommy finds the candy mints in Nana upstairs' sewing box and they eat their candy and talk.

Mrs. S.: Do you have a special drawer, room, box, or cabinet that you can sometimes explore at a relative's or neighbor's house? For instance, when I was a young girl, I used to go into my grandma's pantry. I would slide each drawer open to examine its contents. Sometimes, I would find a little pouch of cinnamon. Another drawer would hold raisins and currants. Yet another might have dried basil or thyme from the banks of the creek behind Grandma's house. (*I open* *my writer's notebook.*) I'm going to make an entry in my writer's notebook about my grandma's pantry and my discoveries. How about you? Do you have any special places that you like to visit or explore?

Madison: My uncle's garage is like that. He's got this huge tool chest. I like to open the drawers and see what's inside.

Leah: My friend's mother lets us look in her jewelry box. We can touch the bracelets and earrings, but we can't put them on.

Felix: My grandpa has a garden shed. Sometimes, we go in there and eat cookies together. No one knows where we are.

Mrs. S.: If any of you would like to make entries in your notebooks about a special place, please take a moment and do that now.

After this demonstration in a second-grade classroom, students selected their ideas for writing workshop. Some students completed a piece of writing already in process. Others chose to write about experiences with relatives and friends. Here are some of their ideas:

- One boy wrote of his special visits to his uncle's house where, at the end of the day, his uncle took a box from his chest of drawers. The uncle placed his war medals across his bed, explaining to the boy the importance of each one. This boy's first draft was filled with reverence for his uncle and his achievements.

- A girl wrote about going to her grandmother's house. On the child's "calm" days, her grandmother opened the hutch and took out her best plates. The girl described how she closed her eyes and ran her fingers around the edges, reading the raised pictures.

- Yet another girl wrote about visiting her friend's house. She told how the house didn't have that many walls to separate the rooms, so the friend's parents had hung fabric. Once in a while, the girl and her friend were allowed to go behind the purple curtain and play with two antique dolls. She explained how fragile the dolls were and how gently she and her friend handled them. She also described the dolls' clothing in great detail.

These students chose to write about extremely personal experiences. I can't say that they wouldn't have thought of these ideas on their own, but I do know that time and time again I see the back-door approach remind students of unique, meaningful events that spark passionate writing.

Great Read-Aloud Series That Provide Ideas

Students in grades 2–4 quite often enjoy reading several books in a series. Sometimes, they follow one character through one conflict after another. Other times, they find a group of books with a format that entertains them in a unique way. Or sometimes, students discover a series that offers them new information about interesting topics. As with single-title literature, you can lead your students into the best book series.

A careful introduction to a series will provide great entertainment and possibly generate more writing ideas, as well. But there is no need to read aloud several titles in a series. Instead, read one or two at the most. Then, let your students know where they can find other books in the series in the classroom, school, or public library.

For instance, I like to read aloud one of the *Magic Tree House* books by Mary Pope Osborne to second graders. Students love these characters and the different predicaments that they encounter as they travel in time and place. After reading aloud the book (this could be first or second reading), I ask one of the following questions:

- How do you think Mary Pope Osborne came up with the idea for this story?

- What if you wanted to write a book similar to this? You wouldn't want to write the very same story, so what could your characters do? Where might they travel? What problem might they face?

The primary reason we read aloud always is for pure enjoyment, so I don't ask a lot of questions, just one or two to gently plant some idea seeds.

Read the Best Books to Produce the Best Ideas

A classroom teacher has such limited time, and there are so many good books to share. I believe it's important to expose students to many different genres. In so doing, we introduce them to a variety of possible writing ideas for the future. In grades 2–4, a teacher has the flexibility to read picture books, news articles, published journals or diary entries, poetry, chapter books, middle-grade novels, and information books and articles.

No matter what kind of print you read to your students, ask one of the following questions:

- How do you think the author came up with the idea for this piece?

- Have you ever had a similar kind of experience? Would you want to write about it?

- Would you want to try this kind of writing someday?

Again, I keep the questions brief and positive. This gives children the power to think and say, "Oh, I could write something like that."

Series Books That Demonstrate Original Ideas

Read one or two of these books throughout the year to introduce original ideas and formats to your students. Then, don't be surprised when they start incorporating similar ideas or designs into their own writing.

- The "Amelia" series by Marissa Moss

- The "American Girl: History Mysteries" series published by Pleasant Co. Publications

- The "Cam Jansen" series by David Adler

- The "Dear America Diaries" series published by Scholastic, Inc.

- The "Let's-Read-And-Find-Out Science" series published by HarperCollins Publishers

- The "Magic School Bus" series by Joanna Cole

- The "Who's Been Here?" series by Lindsay Barrett George

Unique Writing Ideas Chart

As you read a variety of books to students, think about making a chart to record any unique features of the writing. I've used the chart below in many classrooms.

Title	Author	Unique Writing Features/Devices
Magic Tree House	Mary Pope Osborne	Two children travel in their tree house to different places in the world.
When I Was Young in the Mountains	Cynthia Rylant	Lists several memories of a girl and her family when they lived in the Appalachian Mountains.
Home at Last	April Pulley Sayre	Shows how many different animals migrate back home. Includes a repeating line: *home at last.*
Around the Pond: Who's Been Here?	Lindsay Barrett George	Question-and-answer format. Two-page spread of text and illustration shows clues of an animal that has been in the habitat. Reader has the opportunity to decide which animal left the evidence. Next spread shows which animal and what behavior created those clues.
Mathematickles	Betsy Franco	Placing words in mathematical equations, the author creates lively scenes of the four seasons.
Thesaurus Rex	Laya Steinberg	Thesaurus Rex, a dinosaur, introduces readers to synonyms with a rhyming text about his day.
Dear Mrs. LaRue: Letters from Obedience School	Mark Teague	Mrs. LaRue receives letters from her dog, Ike, while he is away at Obedience School. Ike describes the school as harsh and begs to return to his home with her.

Let the Ideas Be Their Own

To encourage students to be inventive and original, they must be given the opportunity to mine their own writing ideas. All teachers in our nation are feeling the pressure to have their students perform well on standardized tests. We do want our students' writing samples to reflect their knowledge and skills. To meet this pressure, some school administrators and teachers are asking them to write in response to prompts too frequently. Repeated use of prompts can extinguish a commitment to writing since this practice prevents students from writing about what they know and care about. Plus, if our ultimate goal is to create independent thinkers and writers who can express themselves, then we must provide daily opportunities for students to use their own ideas so that writing becomes a meaningful experience.

If prompts, story starters, or journal questions are always provided, students become dependent on a given topic and stop thinking for themselves. In my experience, students complain more frequently that they don't know what to write about when they're given a prompt. It makes sense. Not every child can have background experiences or care about teacher- or program-selected topics. Their comments about not knowing what to write may stem from their disinterest in the artificial starter put in front of them.

> "When I've had a fun weekend with my family or friends, I have an idea for a story."
>
> — 3rd grader

It's true that students need to know the procedure for responding to a writing prompt so they are not caught off guard on testing day, however, this practice need not be the gist of our writing workshops. When I work in schools with teachers and students, I suggest that every nine weeks teachers interrupt the regular flow of their writing workshops to give all students the same writing prompt. The kind of prompt, response time, and format can resemble those on standardized tests.

Students want to express themselves. They are eager to learn about craft to improve as writers. They have much to share with an audience. If we as teachers understand this, then we must provide a supportive writing environment that offers students the ability to self-select ideas. We must design mini-lessons on procedures and craft. We must facilitate daily writing time for practice. And, we must make sure that all students receive authentic feedback from an intended audience. It is in this kind of nurturing atmosphere that writers blossom.

We want to encourage choice of ideas so students learn that authentic writing has purpose—that writers write to communicate in a meaningful way with an audience.

Chapter 3 Review

- Exposing students to a wide range of literature gives them permission to write about ideas that are important to them.

- Select books for read-alouds that students can forge emotional connections with.

- Lead students into emotional hot spots in literature so they can remember important moments in their lives to write about.

- Create a chart of unique writing ideas found in published books.

- Rather than offering them prompts, provide opportunities for students to select their own writing ideas on a daily basis .

A Writer's Habit
Keeping a Writer's Notebook

Most adult writers have a bookshelf devoted to their notebooks or journals because we tend to write down anything and everything. One day, when we need that special phrase, idea, or comparison, we'll know where to look— or so we hope.

My notebooks are filled with a variety of entries. Sometimes, I write the summary of a story that delivers itself as a full-length, feature film in a dream. Other times, I hear a snippet of conversation, a humorous name or address, or the title of a book, and I write them down. I might add a photo or a newspaper article that holds promise for future writing. And, of course, I have thousands of ideas, some good and some not, that come from a variety of sources.

Adult writers need notebooks to record their thoughts, ideas, inspirations, and favorite bits of life. Why should student writers be any different? After all, we want them to assume responsibility for their involvement in the writing process. We want them to select their own writing topics— subjects that they care about. We want them to develop the habits of a writer. So, let's make sure that first they have a place to record their thoughts and ideas.

> *"I read, read, read, and then an idea just pops into my head and I write."*
>
> — 2nd grader

A writer's notebook can take many different forms. Some teachers rely on traditional spiral-bound notebooks. Others use black-and-white theme books. Sometimes, teachers staple sheets of paper inside a construction-paper cover. A few teachers ask students to use the back half of their writing workshop book as a notebook. A writing workshop book is typically a large spiral notebook in which a student plans, writes drafts, and revises.

It really doesn't matter what a writer's notebook looks like. What's important is that students have one specific place to record their ideas. Then, we need to make sure they understand the purpose and habit of this writer's tool.

How to Begin a Writer's Notebook

I'm sure there are many effective ways to introduce the use of a writer's notebook, but I can only recommend what I have seen succeed in my own experiences with elementary schoolchildren. In the primary grades K–2, I prefer to begin the year with a community writer's notebook. I buy a large scrapbook and take it into the classroom. The students and I label it "Writer's Notebook." Together, we record writing ideas. I am the scribe, writing down ideas, names, phrases, whatever they want included. The notebook remains out and available to students at all times. They may use it as a resource for ideas or add new ideas as they think of them. Using this notebook builds a common understanding of the purpose of the notebook and how we brainstorm ideas for inclusion. You can use a bulletin board or a large chart paper tablet for the same purpose. In grades 3–12, each individual student can begin the year with his or her own notebook, but the habit of using it needs to be practiced together.

A Different Approach to Brainstorming Ideas

For more years than I would like to admit, I helped students brainstorm writing ideas in two major ways. First, we would list major events that might prove to be interesting writing material. These topics included the following:

- birthdays
- the arrival of a new pet
- summer fun
- an exciting vacation
- the birth of a new brother or sister
- spending the night at a friend's home
- being part of a winning sports team
- the first day of school
- visiting a relative
- building a tent or birdhouse or tree house

There was nothing wrong with this approach. From this type of brainstorming, students usually developed a few strong pieces of writing, some average pieces, and many pieces that needed quite a bit of improvement.

Another way I helped elementary schoolchildren generate writing ideas was from the literature that we read together. We would read books on bears, dolphins, dogs, cats, and deer, and then I expected my students to write a piece about an animal of their choice. I would also read scads of school stories. We'd discuss story structure and brainstorm some school situations together. Then, I would ask them to write their own school stories. Again, a few students wrote strong stories, some wrote average stories, and many were confused and disenchanted with the process.

Today, I help students brainstorm ideas to put into their writer's notebooks by starting with emotions, not events or facts. I begin by explaining the purpose of a writer's notebook to students like this:

> *Writers share something that is important to them with their audience. They work hard at finding just the right words and form to put their thoughts and pictures into the minds of their audience. As writers, we need a place to record what's important to each of us. It's a place to post what we know, what we care about, what interests us. A writer's notebook is personal. What is written inside is different for each writer. Let's begin making entries today of what's important to us.*
>
> *Here is my school writer's notebook. As you can see as I leaf through the pages, I've already written inside. I try to keep my writer's notebook with me at all times so I can make entries when I hear, see, or think of something that I want to record.*

I make sure that my writer's notebook is open and that each student can see it and hear my thinking. Then, I continue:

> *I like to brainstorm through my feelings. We can all remember times when we've been happy, sad, giggly, embarrassed, excited, or angry. I'm going to shut my eyes and remember a time when I was excited.*

I think for a few minutes, trying to come up with three or four different examples that I can offer students. Here's one example.

> *When I was eight years old, there was a large park in town that sold pony rides every Sunday night during the summer and fall. I was so excited when my mom and dad took me there after dinner. I had a favorite pony that was cream-colored with a brown mane. Sometimes, I took five or six rides on him before going home.*
>
> *I'm going to make a note about this in my writer's notebook in case I ever want to write about one of those pony rides.*

Then, students see and hear me writing the following in my notebook: *MacMillan Park—summer and fall of 1958—riding cream-colored pony around the ring—his mane soft in my hands—brown saddle—felt like a princess.*

I point out to students that I'm not writing complete sentences but just enough details to help me remember the emotions of the event later on. I add:

Something I've noticed, and I hope you will, too, is that the more I talk or think about an event, the more details I remember.

Then, I mention another exciting event I remember:

When I was in first grade, we lived in Kentucky for a year because my dad was transferred there for his work. One Saturday morning, my mom and I went window shopping downtown. All of a sudden, the jewelry store window began to wiggle back and forth, and the street shuddered beneath our feet, like it was cold. EARTHQUAKE!
I'm going to add another note about this event.

Again, I make sure students can watch and hear me as I make this entry:

1957—earthquake in Paducah, Kentucky—jewelry store window rattled—displays fell—our images wiggled in the glass—street shuddered—first earthquake of my life—mother held my hand tightly.

At the beginning of the year, I would offer yet a third example. However, as the year progresses, I don't need to be this thorough. Once students understand the process of brainstorming from emotions, they do it without much coaching.

After sharing and recording my ideas, I turn my attention back to students and ask: *Can you remember a time when you were excited?*

They've been thinking all the time I've been brainstorming and writing, so they are ready with their answers.

Usually, for the second emotion, I only have to give one example. Many students are ~ger to share their experiences. I typically call on four or five students. Here are some of ~eir responses about times they've been sad.

- I cried and cried the day my dog got hit by a car and died.
- Last year my grandma was in the nursing home. She looked white and sad and she didn't even remember me.
- My best friend moved away this year. I'll probably never see him again.
- I broke my arm and couldn't play basketball.
- Some older kids made fun of me at recess and it hurt my feelings.
- My mom and dad are getting a divorce. Now I don't know who I'll be living with.
- My best friend doesn't play with me on the playground anymore. I don't know why. It makes me sad because I still like her.

As students share their remembrances, they are filled with passion. These are events ~acked with emotion. Of course, you won't hear a reply to each emotion from every ~udent. The purpose of brainstorming together is to show students what process they ~an use independently to mine ideas for the future.

Be Flexible

From the first day, let students know that if they prefer to brainstorm events or situations from other emotions, they have your blessing. I've always had extremely good success with most students participating with one or both of the emotions that I offer. But just know that one day you may have a student who wants to enter a memory that's generated from an emotion other than the ones you've discussed. After the second emotion, I always say something like this: "If you have another memory that doesn't quite fit into what we've been discussing, please enter that idea into your writer's notebook today."

I have had a few students take me up on that offer. Their faces have shown their relief at having the freedom to write what's on their minds. Remember, we're not offering the different emotions as prompts. We're showing students through example how they can independently generate writing ideas in the future. This strategy is only used in the first two to three weeks of school to provide thorough demonstration and support. Remember to keep the brainstorming time flexible and upbeat throughout the year.

- The day I rode a rollercoaster for the first time.
- When I was named Student-of-the-Week.
- When I got my new bicycle.
- I won the spelling bee last year in my classroom.
- When my baby brother Samuel came home from the hospital.
- I dove off the high-dive at the city pool.
- I watched our dog have seven puppies.
- I jumped in the waves at the ocean.

If we're creating a classroom bulletin board notebook, I might give t[ ] responded a note card or small piece of paper to record their idea, addi[ ] they'd like. Under the heading of EXCITEMENT, we'd post their ideas. [ ] paper or a scrapbook as our first writer's notebook, then I'd act as scrib[ ] their ideas. If students have their own writers' notebooks, then I would [ ] them to add one or more ideas. Many times, students remember a simil[ ] they hear a classmate describe his or her idea.

Providing Choices

On the same day, I would then brainstorm an entirely different set of id[ ] emotion. After all, it would be surprising if everyone that day were in s[ ] enthusiastic mood that they could remember something exciting. So, I [ ] emotion that is quite a bit different than our first choice. I begin this as[ ] in the following way: *Now, let's try and remember a time when we've[ ] think while you think.*

After a few moments I share my thoughts.

> *I remember a year when my father had to take an airplane to [ ] New Jersey, every week to do his job. After Mom and I watched[ ] away on Sunday nights, we were so sad. We knew we'd have t[ ] another five days before seeing him again. Neither one of us s[ ] on the ride home.*

Then, I tell students that I'm going to add that memory to my writer[ ] case I want to write about it some day. As I record the following details[ ] I share them aloud with students:

> *Eleven years old—Dad worked Monday through Friday in Neu[ ] Jersey—flew home on the weekends—had to go back every Sun[ ] Mom and I at Baer Field airport—waved good-bye as his plane[ ] the air—quiet ride all the way back to our house.*

It can be difficult to curb discussion because as students hear the many responses they begin to remember more and more personal situations they want to share. That's a great lead into writer's notebook time. They either can take a few moments and make individual entries into their own notebooks or continue to add notes to the bulletin board, scrapbook, or chart paper.

Fostering the Habit of Writer's Notebook

For the next two weeks, I continue using the different emotions as a catalyst for brainstorming writing ideas. I offer two emotions each day, but students soon understand that they can plug into any emotion that is in the forefront for them. I suggest brainstorming a list of emotions with your students. (The way in which they describe some of the emotions is priceless.) Here are a few to get you started:

- joy
- sadness
- excitement
- anger
- silliness
- disappointment
- pride
- embarrassment
- surprise

I use emotions as the starting point each year, because I believe that to build a writer's community, students need to write about their own lives. Through this writing, they learn more about themselves, one another, and the teacher. Right from the start, we have an emotional investment in each other. Plus, all students have plenty of writing ideas to fuel a successful year of experimentation in the process.

Brainstorming Ideas from Literature

Remember, we can also encourage students to brainstorm ideas from the emotional hot spots in the literature that we read to them each day. What's exciting is watching them discover these pivotal places in the reading themselves. At first, a student will ask to share his or her discovery with the whole class. Later, as more students begin to identify these emotional connections, it becomes a more private celebration, sometimes shared with one or two friends. With practice, this recognition becomes part of the reading process, as well as a way of mining new writing ideas.

Noticing the Unusual

A good friend and professional colleague, Kathy Brita, has her own way of introducing the writer's notebook to her students. She begins by purchasing the smallest spiral notebooks, bound at the top, for each of her students. A local miniature golf course donates small pencils.

During her introduction to writing workshop, Kathy shows her own enthusiasm for the writer's notebook, which she calls a "noticing book." She explains that writers notice the unusual in everything they do. They look at the world with a thoughtful eye.

"We're going to put up our antennae and notice unusual things that we might ordinarily miss," she says while presenting students with their own notebooks. "I want you to notice the sound of trucks coming from the highway, how grass blades point straight up, or how the boarded-up windows of the nearby store look like ghost eyes. But this takes practice, so we'll begin right now with a walk outside."

Before they leave the classroom, Kathy shows students how their noticing books will easily fit inside their hip pockets or the tops of their socks. They take a short walk outside where Kathy points out the unusual, showing students how to stop and observe. She might ask them to squint and describe the shapes they see. She might ask them to look into the distance at the treetops and decide what they look like: pillows? pincushions? soft umbrellas? She might ask them to identify the colors they see in the sky.

On one of their outdoor excursions, Kathy noticed the first "brush" of snow on the ground. "Look!" a boy exclaimed, "the snow is swirling like a snake around my feet." His comment signaled Kathy that the children were indeed beginning to notice the unusual.

Students keep their noticing books with them at school, walking home, on the bus, in the backyard, at the grocery store, at the soccer game, or at ballet class. Kathy encourages them to write not only what they notice around them but also snippets of conversation, interesting words, catchy names of businesses, lines of songs or poetry, even unusual pet names.

Since the books are taken home daily, Kathy asks students to decide on a procedure that will insure the books' return the next day. She asks them what else they always bring to school with them each day. Most years, students say "book bag" or "shoes." But one year, Kathy was surprised when a student said "underwear." It was decided that each night students would lay their noticing books on top of their underwear for the next day. Ironically, no one ever forgot their books that year.

(continued on next page)

Noticing the Unusual

(continued from previous page)

In the classroom, Kathy designates a bulletin board as their large noticing book. At the beginning of the day, she selects six to eight students to share some of what they consider to be their strongest entries. This practice raises awareness among everyone. Hearing what others notice helps them see possibilities where none existed before. Each student who shares entries is asked to post one to three of them on the bulletin board.

Kathy continues this daily practice for two weeks. She knows that she will have to be consistent to establish the habit of using the noticing book. She also continues her modeling by sharing what she adds to her book and posting her "best" on the bulletin board. Then, for the next few weeks, Kathy brings students together once every three to four days. The class adds new observations to the bulletin board. Sometimes, she has students sit with a partner and share what they've noticed. Then, she asks, "Did anyone hear something outstanding that we all need to hear?" This, of course, provides an extra boost to the writer's ego.

Eventually, the students' noticing books grow into wonderful collections of writing ideas. The need for the bulletin board or scrapbook is extinguished. The student writers now have developed a tool that serves them well.

For instance, in *Truman's Aunt Farm* by Jama Kim Rattigan, the author describes how the many aunts fawn over Truman. I've seen a student read this page to friends:

"They all loved Truman and made such a fuss!
'My, how you've grown,' said Aunt Lulu.
'Isn't he handsome?' said Aunt Jodie.
'Looks just like me,' said Aunt Ramona And they hugged him, and patted
his head, and pinched his cheeks, and talked his ears off."

Students giggle when they hear this passage and identify with Truman's plight. When the reader shares that part, the other students nod their heads and call out the "weird" things their relatives do to show affection.

- My uncle always hits my arm when he leaves our house and says, "See ya 'round buddy!"

- My grandma pinches my cheeks, just like in the story, or sometimes she kisses me on the nose.

- My mother always pats my head on top when she sees me in school.

- My grandpa always says, "What's up, boy? I mean besides the sky?"
- My dad twirls me around then he gives me a big hug.

This is great fodder for their writer's notebooks. Maybe students won't plan entire pieces from these descriptions, but they may add these details to future narratives.

Jotting entries and rereading earlier notes needs to become a daily habit for student writers. Don't wait for writing workshop to use the writer's notebook. Show your students that this tool can be a vital resource as they live the life of a writer all day long.

Chapter 4 Review

- A writer's notebook gives students a place to record their writing ideas.
- The teacher brainstorms initial entries into his or her writer's notebook about emotional events from own childhood to use as writing ideas.
- Students must have time to record their writing ideas in their notebooks. They can enter any writing idea that's important to them.
- Foster the use of the writer's notebook throughout the day as students become more observant of what they read and what they observe in the world around them.
- Encourage students to mine writing ideas from literature.

Maintaining Momentum with the Notebook

After working with the notebooks for these first weeks, it's time to show students other ways to brainstorm ideas to include in them. Of course, the best way to do this is through your own day-to-day modeling. Show students how to observe the world and notice the unusual or unique; how to wonder about their world and write entries for investigations; how to listen to conversations and record interesting passages and gestures; how to examine personal artifacts and note their importance; how to list book or movie titles, favorite foods, or the qualities of a friend; and how to record words they want to add to their writing vocabularies. Don't attempt all of this in a week or a month. Ease into the use of the writer's notebook, and help your students explore all their possible ideas throughout the school year.

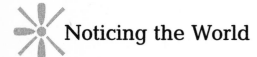

Noticing the World

Writers are thinkers, and thinkers are reflective, observant people. Help your students take the time to really be a part of their environment. Teaching them to slow down, to stop and observe the world around them is so rewarding. However, you need to start out slowly and model how to do this. Just as Kathy Brita assists her students in noticing the unusual (see Chapter 4, pages 34–35), you, too, will want to help your students observe what they might have missed in their environment.

I like to start with objects in the classroom. For instance, I might bring in a bouquet of flowers and say the following: *Let's all look at these chrysanthemums. We can see that they are gold in color. But what does that color look like? How could we describe it without just saying it's gold? For instance, I could say: "The flowers beam gold like ripe wheat in the afternoon sun." Now, you look at the chrysanthemums and think about how you could describe them. Be bold. Think out of the box.*

These are a few responses I've heard from students:

- The flowers are the color of butter melting on corn-on-the-cob.
- The chrysanthemums look like candlelight.
- The flowers are the same color as my canary.
- The end of each stem has a gold coin opening up.

If I want to stretch students a bit further, I might choose another common object in the classroom and say: *Look at the alphabet above the blackboard. There are two examples of all twenty-six letters. Now, we know that the letters are printed on paper and the paper is not going anywhere, but a writer tries to paint pictures. Look at them, and pretend they are moving. What might they be doing? For instance, I could say: "Twenty-six letters are dancing in a conga line over the chalkboard." Take a moment and decide what they look like they're doing to you.*

Students always surprise me with their answers. Here are a few samples:

- They're marching above the chalkboard.
- The alphabet is parading over the wall.
- They're tiptoeing from one end to the other.
- Twenty-six letters play follow-the-leader.

Our ideas are often filled with poetic or descriptive language as we look for the unusual. Just like Kathy Brita with her noticing books, you might take your students outside and train their senses so they see, hear, smell, or touch in new ways. After three or four practice sessions, they will independently be more observant of their world. They'll notice how the cafeteria lady's freckles are darker when her face is hot from the kitchen. Someone will mention that your left foot always bounces up and down when you're writing. They might even comment on how they can hear squeaks and squeals like those of a trapped animal when the flag is raised outside on the flagpole each morning.

Again, these observations alone are not writing ideas, but they could one day lead to a piece of writing. Or they might be details that will find their way into a poem, story, or descriptive piece.

 ## Wondering About the World

Another way to help your students brainstorm writing ideas for their notebooks is by posing this question: *What do you wonder about? In other words, what makes you think **how** or **why**?*

Again, you need to model with the questions you wonder about and would like answered. Here are a few of my wonderings:

- I wonder how bees know where to fly to find nectar and collect pollen.
- I wonder how long it takes for water that starts at the source of the Mississippi River to travel to the Gulf of Mexico.
- I wonder how my body would feel if I ran twenty minutes without stopping.

- I wonder what it would be like to time travel. What if I could walk down the basement steps and be back in colonial America.? What would I do? Where would I live?
- I wonder how many different books I've read so far this year.
- I wonder what exactly happened to Amelia Earhart after her plane went down in the Pacific Ocean.

First Pages From a Third Grader's Writer's Notebook

* How I spent my time during a lightning storm—power flickered off and on—read, colored with markers, played Sorry, made a craft bowl

* Florida trip—flew on a plane—seat 5—snack lady

* Rules for a Spelling Bee—study, write your name on paper, 2 pencils, use dividers, listen to directions

* 6th birthday and Wizard of Oz theme—friends, clown named Oppie, balloon flower, cake

* Soccer game—must have accessories—long, black socks, cleats, shin guards, and teammates, different positions, teamwork

* Binder Park Zoo—animals, bridges, trees, feed animals, licking, long tongues, biscuit treats, gift shop, train and tunnel

* No! poem—no writing, history, attitude just soccer

* Neighborhood garden—Partridge Woods, big area between houses— take turns taking care of it—watering, cover seeds, planting flowers and watermelon, carrots, strawberries

* Pet gerbil—Peanut—left Petco and got his stuff—nervous cried, he wasn't there—SOLD!

In your modeling, you need to show that any kind of question is worthwhile, as long as it's something that you sincerely care to know. Sometimes, these wonderings may lead to the writing of an informational piece. Other times, they may lead to a piece of science fiction, poetry, or personal narrative. The wondering and questioning is simply a starting point. Students have an endless supply of curiosity and questions. They will enjoy adding these kinds of entries to their notebooks.

Listening to the World

As we help students become more observant, they will automatically become better listeners. To enhance their enjoyment of this skill, I tell them: *We're going to be conversation spies. A writer is always listening to see how people speak and what exactly they say. A good spy eavesdrops without letting people know that he or she is there. In your spying, notice the exact words people say that show surprise, anger, concern, grief, joy, confusion, or worry. Notice their body language, how they move, as well as what they say. All of this will help you write authentic scenes between characters.*

Again, you want to show your students some clips of conversations that you have overheard and recorded in your writer's notebook. Here are some bits of overheard conversation on a weekend trip to Chicago that I've shared with students:

- "The camera's gone!" said the woman, pawing through her purse. "Do you think I left it somewhere? When did I last use it? Do you think someone took it?"

- "Is the three o'clock tour the same as the architectural cruise?" asked a woman, walking up to the ticket booth.
  "Well," said a man, nodding up the river. "It's a cruise and we talk about architecture on the river."

- "Look!" shouted the young boy. "It's a shark—a mean one."
  "How can you tell that it's mean?" asked his mother.
  "His eyes—see how he looks at me!" said the boy, pointing up at the fish.
  "He's mean."

Suggest that your students take their notebooks with them into the lunchroom and out at recess. They'll want the notebooks handy when they hear those snippets that show emotion. Remind students that they don't have to write down everything that is said— only the parts that seem to be central to the exchange or the emotion.

Sketches and Photographs of the World

Pictures are invaluable to a writer. Many adult writers sketch characters, wildlife, flowers, or settings in their notebooks. They do this so the image cannot fade. If they want to remember how the tulip petals looked as if they were praying, they may draw a sketch.

If they want to remember Aunt Helen's new hat, they may photograph it. Writers include sketches, photographs, magazine illustrations, and cartoons in their notebooks to remind them of unforgettable people, places, and things.

Without a doubt, most students are better artists than I. They always enjoy sketching a variety of images in their notebooks. I've seen plenty of dogs and cats and hamsters peeking from their pages. Students sometimes add logos or symbols, their own original cartoon characters, or sketches of cars or buildings. When a student takes the time to illustrate, you can believe he or she is interested in that subject matter. You'll probably notice the child returning to that same subject many times throughout the year.

Then there are some students, like me, who are not great sketch artists. You can suggest they bring in illustrations from magazines or photographs from the newspaper that show people, places, and things that they might like to write about. Also, encourage students to bring in a few photographs that show a time when they were happy, sad, excited, surprised, or amazed. Have them place these photos in their notebooks with a note or two about their importance. These photos and captions can be great catalysts for future writing.

> *"I watch movies. They give me ideas for new characters and plots."*
>
> — 4th grader

Artifacts from Their World

What did you collect as a child? I had jars filled with rocks—smooth rocks, colorful rocks, rocks that looked like hearts. I also collected stamps from around the world, each in its own tissue-paper envelope. Many of our students have collections, too. You can encourage them to bring in artifacts that represent their collections. These items fascinate students and show a part of them that most of their classmates don't know. Such artifacts can be attached to their notebooks with a comment or two, or students may show friends their artifacts and simply write a description or other interesting information in their notebooks. Students might want to make a rubbing of the artifact and place it in their notebook, or they might put items in zip-lock bags to staple inside its pages.

Besides collections, other artifacts might remind students of writing ideas. They might bring in napkins or menus from restaurants where they've had memorable meals, a playbill from a class trip to the theater, or a ticket stub from a museum. Someone might include a piece of a collar from a lost pet. As a child, I probably would have included a fried marble from my jewelry-making days or a woven potholder as a reminder of how much money I made selling them door to door. Whatever the artifacts, they add new lifeblood to students' notebooks by providing completely different entries for future reference.

Lists

As a wife, mother, writer, teacher, and speaker, I must create eight to twelve lists a week. Some lists repeat themselves: grocery lists, to-do lists, my writing goals, materials to prepare for presentations. Other lists are only necessary once in a while: book titles that make excellent read-alouds in kindergarten, people to contact for a small dinner party, materials needed to renovate my office, museums to visit while in a particular city. I also have fun lists—lists that support my dreams: islands I want to visit someday, future books I'm eager to write, new foods I want to cook or bake, new herbs or perennials to add to my gardens. If it wasn't important to me, I wouldn't take the time to make a list.

Your students have responsibilities and dreams, too. Encourage them to enter lists into their notebooks—especially about people, places, and things they care about. Here are some examples of what some of my students have listed:

- all the ways my sister bugs me
- my top ten favorite books of all time
- all the tricks my dog can do
- summertime treats
- noises I can hear from my bed at night
- the games I love most at recess
- what I've hidden in the back of my closet
- bugs and animals that scare me
- animals that I'd like to see in person
- all the states I've visited or driven through
- my five least favorite household chores

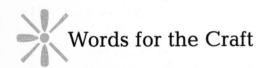

Words for the Craft

You and your students may designate a particular place in your notebooks for special words. One list may be words that are fun to say, like *ricochet, teensy, Katmandu,* or *perpendicular*. Another list may be words that you or your students want to add to your working vocabulary: *superimpose, flabbergasted, catapulted,* or *redemption*. Another list may be quirky words like *facetious* (a word that has all the vowels in *a, e, i, o, u* order) or *vacuum* that has two *u*'s next to one another, or *queue* (a word that is pronounced like its first letter).

I usually talk about word choice when visiting schools as an author. I often ask students to name words that fit into one of these categories. I'm always surprised by the number of answers I receive. Even in schools where teachers admit they've never identified words accordingly, students have ready replies. You can tell that students have been fascinated with certain words and are anxious to share their favorites.

I always tell students that writers are wordsmiths. Just as a blacksmith uses metals as a natural resource, a writer uses words. Wordsmiths collect words, know words, celebrate words, and are always on the look out for new and exciting ones to add to their working vocabularies. The notebook is one place that students can list words for future reference.

Nurturing the Notebook's Use

Making the writer's notebook a habit is only the beginning. Just like the other aspects of the writing process, you need to nurture its use. Continue to consult with the students at least once a week throughout the year. Ask them these kinds of questions about their notebooks to keep their engagement high:

- What helps you the most to continue to record entries in your notebook?

- Have you added something new to your notebook that might be helpful to share with others?

- Which parts of your notebook do you refer to the most?

- Which parts of your notebook do you refer to the least?

- Have you become more observant? Tell me how.

- Do you always consult your notebook before starting a new piece of writing or only some of the time?

- If you were going to give advice to a student writer who was just beginning a writer's notebook, what would that advice be?

Taking Writer's Notebooks One Step Further

Ralph Fletcher has written a wonderful book entitled *A Writer's Notebook: Unlocking the Writer Within You*. This book can help you and your students brainstorm different kinds of entries for their notebooks such as the following:

- lists of people you admire
- scenes from dreams
- memories of birthdays
- artifacts like seashells or letters

The author shows that each writer's notebook will be unique. It's a place for a writer to record his or her reactions to everything personal in the world.

Mr. Fletcher says, "A writer's notebook gives you a place to live like a writer, not just in school during writing time, but wherever you are, at any time of day."

I recommend reading parts of this book out loud to your class. Each day, conduct a mini-workshop around a new chapter. Ask students their opinions about Mr. Fletcher's comments and recommendations. If you want your students to be involved, include them in the process, beginning with professional reading. Then, sit back and watch your student writers live in their notebooks.

We know that each student's notebook will look a little different because of its personal nature, but I've noticed that notebooks even look quite a bit different from classroom to classroom. Some teachers ask their students to save the last fifteen or twenty pages as a toolbox so they can make brief notes or write examples from mini-lessons, add revision strategies, or list all the ways they can independently edit their writing for spelling and punctuation. Some students have examples of "show, not tell" so they will be able to recognize the difference in their own writing.

A Cautionary Note: Don't burden the writer's notebook with too many classroom procedures and rules. The charm and appeal of the notebook is that it belongs to the student; it's a private place where a student can live and think like a writer. If we intrude too often into those pages, no matter how good our intentions, we run the risk of extinguishing all commitment to the notebook and its enjoyment and use.

> *"I write about my favorites things like cats, the rainforest, and the beach."*
>
> — 4th grader

Modeling a Notebook's Use

We should always practice what we preach. We show students how to multiply by modeling it on the blackboard. We show them how to draw diagrams by drawing the figures ourselves on the overhead projector. We model how to use grammar correctly by speaking well in front of students. Therefore, if we want to show them that we value original ideas, then we need to model how we select ideas for our own writing.

I've mentioned before that my writer's notebook is always with me when I'm brainstorming writing ideas with students. As classroom teachers, our writers' notebooks always need to be out on our desks, available when an idea hits us. Our students also need to see us record those inspired ideas that come out of nowhere.

Maybe you notice something at the window of the classroom, and you make an entry in your notebook: *cardinal's red fluttered past the window, like a Valentine in flight.* Or perhaps you hear one of your students say something—a clip of conversation that catches your ear, and you write it down: *My mom's violin practice scratches my ears.* You might see the humorous name of a beauty salon while on a weekend trip. Show students that you wanted to remember the name, so you wrote it in your notebook in case you ever needed a funny name in a story: *Bab's Bob & Bounce.*

Every time we make another entry in our notebooks, we are showing students that we value this tool and the role it plays in the writing process.

Chapter 5 Review

- Help students observe and describe the world around them.
- Encourage students to add questions they have about the world to their notebooks.
- Guide students in listening for bits of conversation to include in their notebooks.
- Show students how to include photos, sketches, or symbols in their notebooks
- Suggest that students include artifacts, or notes about them, in their notebooks
- Students can write lists of words, favorites things, and books they've read in their notebooks.
- Revisit the notebooks at least once a week during the year.
- Maintain your notebook in front of students during the year to highlight its place as the constant tool of writer.

Final Thoughts: A Lifetime Habit

The wonderful advantage of using writer's notebooks in your classroom instead of story starters, topic lists, or daily prompts is that you are leading students into one of the lifetime habits of a writer—a real writer—not just someone who tries to write well on standardized tests. You are providing children with a gift by teaching them how to slow down, stop, and observe the world around them. You're modeling how thinkers reflect and find the unusual. As you and your students develop into a community of writers, you'll notice how much lengthier their entries become.

You'll also notice how anxious students are to write everyday: They now have a tool teeming with writing ideas, and it grows faster than they can write. The notebooks fuel an excitement that will carry all of you through the year and beyond. Be brave. Take the first steps with your students and read, think, brainstorm, talk, record, and live like writers—because you are.

"I like to write poetry. My ideas come from nature. I add details and description."
— 4th grader

Bibliography

Adler, David A. "Cam Jansen Mysteries." New York: Penguin Putnam Books for Young Readers.

Allard, Harry G. *Miss Nelson Is Missing.* Boston: Houghton Mifflin & Co., 1977.

"American Girl: History Mysteries." Middleton, WI: Pleasant Company Publications.

Bang, Molly. *When Sophie Gets Angry—Really, Really Angry.* New York: Scholastic, 1999.

Bunting, Eve. *The Memory String.* New York: Clarion Books, 2000.

Cheney, Lynne. *A Is for Abigail.* New York: Simon & Schuster, 2003.

Cole, Joanna. "Magic School Bus" books. New York: Scholastic, Inc.

Cronin, Doreen. *Diary of a Worm.* New York: HarperCollins, 2003.

Curtis, Jamie Lee. *Today I Feel Silly and Other Moods That Make My Day.* New York: HarperCollins, 1998.

"Dear America Diaries." New York: Scholastic, Inc.

dePaola, Tomie. *Nana Upstairs & Nana Downstairs.* New York: Putnam's Sons, 1973.

Dotlich, Rebecca Kai. *Mama Loves.* New York: HarperCollins, 2004.

Ehlert, Lois. *Waiting for Wings.* San Diego: Harcourt, Inc. 2001.

Ewart, Claire. *Fossil.* New York: Walker and Company, 2004.

Fletcher, Ralph. *A Writer's Notebook: Unlocking the Writer Within You*. New York: Avon Books, Inc., 1996.

Franco, Betsy. *Mathematickles*. New York: Simon & Schuster Children's Books, 2003.

George, Lindsay Barrett. "Who's Been Here? books. New York: Greenwillow Books, HarperCollins.

High, Linda Oatman. *Barn Savers*. Honesdale, PA: Boyds Mills Press, 1999.

High, Linda Oatman. *The Girl on the High-Diving Horse: An Adventure in Atlantic City*. New York: Philomel Books, 2003.

Hoffman, Mary. *Amazing Grace*. New York: Dial Books for Young Readers, 1991.

Koehler-Pentacoff, Elizabeth. *The ABC's of Writing for Children*. Sanger, CA: Quill Driver Books/Word Dancer Press, Inc., 2003.

"Let's-Read-And-Find-Out Science" books. New York: HarperCollins Publishers.

MacLachlan, Patricia. *Journey*. New York: Delacorte Press, 1991.

Martin, Jacqueline Briggs. *On Sand Island*. Boston: Houghton Mifflin, 2003.

Moss, Marissa. The "Amelia" books. Middleton, WI: Pleasant Company Publications.

Osborne, Mary Pope. "The Magic Tree House" books. New York: Random House.

Peters, Lisa Westberg. *Earthshake: Poems from the Ground Up*. New York: Greenwillow, 2003.

Polacco, Patricia. *Thank You, Mr. Falker*. New York: Philomel Books, 1998.

Rattigan, Jama Kim. *Truman's Aunt Farm*. Boston: Houghton Mifflin Co., 1994.

Richards, Jean. *How the Elephant Got Its Trunk*. New York: Henry Holt and Company, 2003.

Rosenberry, Vera. *Vera Runs Away*. New York: Henry Holt and Company, 2000.

Rosenberry, Vera. *When Vera Was Sick.* New York: Henry Holt and Company, 1998.

Ryan, Pam Munoz. *How Do You Raise a Raisin?* Watertown, MA: Charlesbridge Publishing, 2003.

Rylant, Cynthia. *The Relatives Came.* New York: Bradbury Press, 1985.

Rylant, Cynthia. *When I Was Young in the Mountains.* New York: E. P. Dutton, 1982.

St. George, Judith. *So You Want to Be an Inventor?* New York: Philomel, 2002.

Sayre, April Pulley. *Home at Last.* New York: Henry Holt and Company, 1998.

Sayre, April Pulley. *One Is a Snail, Ten Is a Crab.* Cambridge, MA: Candlewick Press, 2003.

Steinberg, Laya. *Thesaurus Rex.* Cambridge, MA: Barefoot Books, 2003.

Stewart, Sarah. *The Gardener.* New York: Farrar.Straus.Giroux, 1997.

Teague, Mark. *Dear Mrs. LaRue: Letters from Obedience School.* New York: Scholastic, 2002.

Wiles, Deborah. *Freedom Summer.* New York: Atheneum Books for Young Readers, 2001.